Scale Verification Issue Page

Book Number _____

Issued To: _____

Department /
Organization _____

Issued On: _____

Returned On: _____

Notes: _____

_____

_____

_____

_____

_____

_____

_____

Book Instructions

1. Calibrate scales on a weekly basis and record the calibration weight and corrective action taken, if applicable, within the log book.

2. Employees will verify that production operators are using the scales properly by making visual observations of employee activities during all hours of operation.

3. Log book should be reviewed and initial weekly.

4. Maintain this log for a minimum of 1 year.

5. Use ink; do not erase; delete any mistakes by neatly drawing a single line through it

6. Do not remove pages, and do not skip pages

Notable Items / Description (if any)	Page

Notable Items / Description (if any)	Page

Scale Verification Log

Date	Scale Being Calibrated	Test Weight		Corrective Action	Initials
		Example 200 g / 2 kg	Example 500 g / 4 kg		

Reviewed by (printed name)	Reviewed by (signature)	Date

Scale Verification Log

Date	Scale Being Calibrated	Test Weight		Corrective Action	Initials
		Example 200 g / 2 kg	Example 500 g / 4 kg		

Reviewed by (printed name)	Reviewed by (signature)	Date

Scale Verification Log

Date	Scale Being Calibrated	Test Weight		Corrective Action	Initials
		Example 200 g / 2 kg	Example 500 g / 4 kg		

Reviewed by (printed name)	Reviewed by (signature)	Date

Scale Verification Log

Date	Scale Being Calibrated	Test Weight		Corrective Action	Initials
		Example 200 g / 2 kg	Example 500 g / 4 kg		

Reviewed by (printed name)	Reviewed by (signature)	Date

Scale Verification Log

Date	Scale Being Calibrated	Test Weight		Corrective Action	Initials
		Example 200 g / 2 kg	Example 500 g / 4 kg		

Reviewed by (printed name)	Reviewed by (signature)	Date

Scale Verification Log

Date	Scale Being Calibrated	Test Weight		Corrective Action	Initials
		Example 200 g / 2 kg	Example 500 g / 4 kg		

Reviewed by (printed name)	Reviewed by (signature)	Date

Scale Verification Log

Date	Scale Being Calibrated	Test Weight		Corrective Action	Initials
		Example 200 g / 2 kg	Example 500 g / 4 kg		

Reviewed by (printed name)	Reviewed by (signature)	Date

Scale Verification Log

Date	Scale Being Calibrated	Test Weight		Corrective Action	Initials
		Example 200 g / 2 kg	Example 500 g / 4 kg		

Reviewed by (printed name)	Reviewed by (signature)	Date

Scale Verification Log

Date	Scale Being Calibrated	Test Weight		Corrective Action	Initials
		Example 200 g / 2 kg	Example 500 g / 4 kg		

Reviewed by (printed name)	Reviewed by (signature)	Date

Scale Verification Log

Date	Scale Being Calibrated	Test Weight		Corrective Action	Initials
		Example 200 g / 2 kg	Example 500 g / 4 kg		

Reviewed by (printed name)	Reviewed by (signature)	Date

Scale Verification Log

Date	Scale Being Calibrated	Test Weight		Corrective Action	Initials
		Example 200 g / 2 kg	Example 500 g / 4 kg		

Reviewed by (printed name)	Reviewed by (signature)	Date

Scale Verification Log

Date	Scale Being Calibrated	Test Weight		Corrective Action	Initials
		Example 200 g / 2 kg	Example 500 g / 4 kg		

Reviewed by (printed name)	Reviewed by (signature)	Date

Scale Verification Log

Date	Scale Being Calibrated	Test Weight		Corrective Action	Initials
		Example 200 g / 2 kg	Example 500 g / 4 kg		

Reviewed by (printed name)	Reviewed by (signature)	Date

Scale Verification Log

Date	Scale Being Calibrated	Test Weight		Corrective Action	Initials
		Example 200 g / 2 kg	Example 500 g / 4 kg		

Reviewed by (printed name)	Reviewed by (signature)	Date

Scale Verification Log

Date	Scale Being Calibrated	Test Weight		Corrective Action	Initials
		Example 200 g / 2 kg	Example 500 g / 4 kg		

Reviewed by (printed name)	Reviewed by (signature)	Date

Scale Verification Log

Date	Scale Being Calibrated	Test Weight		Corrective Action	Initials
		Example 200 g / 2 kg	Example 500 g / 4 kg		

Reviewed by (printed name)	Reviewed by (signature)	Date

Scale Verification Log

Date	Scale Being Calibrated	Test Weight		Corrective Action	Initials
		Example 200 g / 2 kg	Example 500 g / 4 kg		

Reviewed by (printed name)	Reviewed by (signature)	Date

Scale Verification Log

Date	Scale Being Calibrated	Test Weight		Corrective Action	Initials
		Example 200 g / 2 kg	Example 500 g / 4 kg		

Reviewed by (printed name)	Reviewed by (signature)	Date

Scale Verification Log

Date	Scale Being Calibrated	Test Weight		Corrective Action	Initials
		Example 200 g / 2 kg	Example 500 g / 4 kg		

Reviewed by (printed name)	Reviewed by (signature)	Date

Scale Verification Log

Date	Scale Being Calibrated	Test Weight		Corrective Action	Initials
		Example 200 g / 2 kg	Example 500 g / 4 kg		

Reviewed by (printed name)	Reviewed by (signature)	Date

Scale Verification Log

Date	Scale Being Calibrated	Test Weight		Corrective Action	Initials
		Example 200 g / 2 kg	Example 500 g / 4 kg		

Reviewed by (printed name)	Reviewed by (signature)	Date

Scale Verification Log

Date	Scale Being Calibrated	Test Weight		Corrective Action	Initials
		Example 200 g / 2 kg	Example 500 g / 4 kg		

Reviewed by (printed name)	Reviewed by (signature)	Date

Scale Verification Log

Date	Scale Being Calibrated	Test Weight		Corrective Action	Initials
		Example 200 g / 2 kg	Example 500 g / 4 kg		

Reviewed by (printed name)	Reviewed by (signature)	Date

Scale Verification Log

Date	Scale Being Calibrated	Test Weight		Corrective Action	Initials
		Example 200 g / 2 kg	Example 500 g / 4 kg		

Reviewed by (printed name)	Reviewed by (signature)	Date

Scale Verification Log

Date	Scale Being Calibrated	Test Weight		Corrective Action	Initials
		Example 200 g / 2 kg	Example 500 g / 4 kg		

Reviewed by (printed name)	Reviewed by (signature)	Date

Scale Verification Log

Date	Scale Being Calibrated	Test Weight		Corrective Action	Initials
		Example 200 g / 2 kg	Example 500 g / 4 kg		

Reviewed by (printed name)	Reviewed by (signature)	Date

Scale Verification Log

Date	Scale Being Calibrated	Test Weight		Corrective Action	Initials
		Example 200 g / 2 kg	Example 500 g / 4 kg		

Reviewed by (printed name)	Reviewed by (signature)	Date

Scale Verification Log

Date	Scale Being Calibrated	Test Weight		Corrective Action	Initials
		Example 200 g / 2 kg	Example 500 g / 4 kg		

Reviewed by (printed name)	Reviewed by (signature)	Date

Scale Verification Log

Date	Scale Being Calibrated	Test Weight		Corrective Action	Initials
		Example 200 g / 2 kg	Example 500 g / 4 kg		

Reviewed by (printed name)	Reviewed by (signature)	Date

Scale Verification Log

Date	Scale Being Calibrated	Test Weight		Corrective Action	Initials
		Example 200 g / 2 kg	Example 500 g / 4 kg		

Reviewed by (printed name)	Reviewed by (signature)	Date

Scale Verification Log

Date	Scale Being Calibrated	Test Weight		Corrective Action	Initials
		Example 200 g / 2 kg	Example 500 g / 4 kg		

Reviewed by (printed name)	Reviewed by (signature)	Date

Scale Verification Log

Date	Scale Being Calibrated	Test Weight		Corrective Action	Initials
		Example 200 g / 2 kg	Example 500 g / 4 kg		

Reviewed by (printed name)	Reviewed by (signature)	Date

Scale Verification Log

Date	Scale Being Calibrated	Test Weight		Corrective Action	Initials
		Example 200 g / 2 kg	Example 500 g / 4 kg		

Reviewed by (printed name)	Reviewed by (signature)	Date

Scale Verification Log

Date	Scale Being Calibrated	Test Weight		Corrective Action	Initials
		Example 200 g / 2 kg	Example 500 g / 4 kg		

Reviewed by (printed name)	Reviewed by (signature)	Date

Scale Verification Log

Date	Scale Being Calibrated	Test Weight		Corrective Action	Initials
		Example 200 g / 2 kg	Example 500 g / 4 kg		

Reviewed by (printed name)	Reviewed by (signature)	Date

Scale Verification Log

Date	Scale Being Calibrated	Test Weight		Corrective Action	Initials
		Example 200 g / 2 kg	Example 500 g / 4 kg		

Reviewed by (printed name)	Reviewed by (signature)	Date

Scale Verification Log

Date	Scale Being Calibrated	Test Weight		Corrective Action	Initials
		Example 200 g / 2 kg	Example 500 g / 4 kg		

Reviewed by (printed name)	Reviewed by (signature)	Date

Scale Verification Log

Date	Scale Being Calibrated	Test Weight		Corrective Action	Initials
		Example 200 g / 2 kg	Example 500 g / 4 kg		

Reviewed by (printed name)	Reviewed by (signature)	Date

Scale Verification Log

Date	Scale Being Calibrated	Test Weight		Corrective Action	Initials
		Example 200 g / 2 kg	Example 500 g / 4 kg		

Reviewed by (printed name)	Reviewed by (signature)	Date

Scale Verification Log

Date	Scale Being Calibrated	Test Weight		Corrective Action	Initials
		Example 200 g / 2 kg	Example 500 g / 4 kg		

Reviewed by (printed name)	Reviewed by (signature)	Date

Scale Verification Log

Date	Scale Being Calibrated	Test Weight		Corrective Action	Initials
		Example 200 g / 2 kg	Example 500 g / 4 kg		

Reviewed by (printed name)	Reviewed by (signature)	Date

Scale Verification Log

Date	Scale Being Calibrated	Test Weight		Corrective Action	Initials
		Example 200 g / 2 kg	Example 500 g / 4 kg		

Reviewed by (printed name)	Reviewed by (signature)	Date

Scale Verification Log

Date	Scale Being Calibrated	Test Weight		Corrective Action	Initials
		Example 200 g / 2 kg	Example 500 g / 4 kg		

Reviewed by (printed name)	Reviewed by (signature)	Date

Scale Verification Log

Date	Scale Being Calibrated	Test Weight		Corrective Action	Initials
		Example 200 g / 2 kg	Example 500 g / 4 kg		

Reviewed by (printed name)	Reviewed by (signature)	Date

Scale Verification Log

Date	Scale Being Calibrated	Test Weight		Corrective Action	Initials
		Example 200 g / 2 kg	Example 500 g / 4 kg		

Reviewed by (printed name)	Reviewed by (signature)	Date

Scale Verification Log

Date	Scale Being Calibrated	Test Weight		Corrective Action	Initials
		Example 200 g / 2 kg	Example 500 g / 4 kg		

Reviewed by (printed name)	Reviewed by (signature)	Date

Scale Verification Log

Date	Scale Being Calibrated	Test Weight		Corrective Action	Initials
		Example 200 g / 2 kg	Example 500 g / 4 kg		

Reviewed by (printed name)	Reviewed by (signature)	Date

Scale Verification Log

Date	Scale Being Calibrated	Test Weight		Corrective Action	Initials
		Example 200 g / 2 kg	Example 500 g / 4 kg		

Reviewed by (printed name)	Reviewed by (signature)	Date

Scale Verification Log

Date	Scale Being Calibrated	Test Weight		Corrective Action	Initials
		Example 200 g / 2 kg	Example 500 g / 4 kg		

Reviewed by (printed name)	Reviewed by (signature)	Date

Scale Verification Log

Date	Scale Being Calibrated	Test Weight		Corrective Action	Initials
		Example 200 g / 2 kg	Example 500 g / 4 kg		

Reviewed by (printed name)	Reviewed by (signature)	Date

Scale Verification Log

Date	Scale Being Calibrated	Test Weight		Corrective Action	Initials
		Example 200 g / 2 kg	Example 500 g / 4 kg		

Reviewed by (printed name)	Reviewed by (signature)	Date

Scale Verification Log

Date	Scale Being Calibrated	Test Weight		Corrective Action	Initials
		Example 200 g / 2 kg	Example 500 g / 4 kg		

Reviewed by (printed name)	Reviewed by (signature)	Date

Scale Verification Log

Date	Scale Being Calibrated	Test Weight		Corrective Action	Initials
		Example 200 g / 2 kg	Example 500 g / 4 kg		

Reviewed by (printed name)	Reviewed by (signature)	Date

Scale Verification Log

Date	Scale Being Calibrated	Test Weight		Corrective Action	Initials
		Example 200 g / 2 kg	Example 500 g / 4 kg		

Reviewed by (printed name)	Reviewed by (signature)	Date

Scale Verification Log

Date	Scale Being Calibrated	Test Weight		Corrective Action	Initials
		Example 200 g / 2 kg	Example 500 g / 4 kg		

Reviewed by (printed name)	Reviewed by (signature)	Date

Scale Verification Log

Date	Scale Being Calibrated	Test Weight		Corrective Action	Initials
		Example 200 g / 2 kg	Example 500 g / 4 kg		

Reviewed by (printed name)	Reviewed by (signature)	Date

Scale Verification Log

Date	Scale Being Calibrated	Test Weight		Corrective Action	Initials
		Example 200 g / 2 kg	Example 500 g / 4 kg		

Reviewed by (printed name)	Reviewed by (signature)	Date

Scale Verification Log

Date	Scale Being Calibrated	Test Weight		Corrective Action	Initials
		Example 200 g / 2 kg	Example 500 g / 4 kg		

Reviewed by (printed name)	Reviewed by (signature)	Date

Scale Verification Log

Date	Scale Being Calibrated	Test Weight		Corrective Action	Initials
		Example 200 g / 2 kg	Example 500 g / 4 kg		

Reviewed by (printed name)	Reviewed by (signature)	Date

Scale Verification Log

Date	Scale Being Calibrated	Test Weight		Corrective Action	Initials
		Example 200 g / 2 kg	Example 500 g / 4 kg		

Reviewed by (printed name)	Reviewed by (signature)	Date

Scale Verification Log

Date	Scale Being Calibrated	Test Weight		Corrective Action	Initials
		Example 200 g / 2 kg	Example 500 g / 4 kg		

Reviewed by (printed name)	Reviewed by (signature)	Date

Scale Verification Log

Date	Scale Being Calibrated	Test Weight		Corrective Action	Initials
		Example 200 g / 2 kg	Example 500 g / 4 kg		

Reviewed by (printed name)	Reviewed by (signature)	Date

Scale Verification Log

Date	Scale Being Calibrated	Test Weight		Corrective Action	Initials
		Example 200 g / 2 kg	Example 500 g / 4 kg		

Reviewed by (printed name)	Reviewed by (signature)	Date

Scale Verification Log

Date	Scale Being Calibrated	Test Weight		Corrective Action	Initials
		Example 200 g / 2 kg	Example 500 g / 4 kg		

Reviewed by (printed name)	Reviewed by (signature)	Date

Scale Verification Log

Date	Scale Being Calibrated	Test Weight		Corrective Action	Initials
		Example 200 g / 2 kg	Example 500 g / 4 kg		

Reviewed by (printed name)	Reviewed by (signature)	Date

Scale Verification Log

Date	Scale Being Calibrated	Test Weight		Corrective Action	Initials
		Example 200 g / 2 kg	Example 500 g / 4 kg		

Reviewed by (printed name)	Reviewed by (signature)	Date

Scale Verification Log

Date	Scale Being Calibrated	Test Weight		Corrective Action	Initials
		Example 200 g / 2 kg	Example 500 g / 4 kg		

Reviewed by (printed name)	Reviewed by (signature)	Date

Scale Verification Log

Date	Scale Being Calibrated	Test Weight		Corrective Action	Initials
		Example 200 g / 2 kg	Example 500 g / 4 kg		

Reviewed by (printed name)	Reviewed by (signature)	Date

Scale Verification Log

Date	Scale Being Calibrated	Test Weight		Corrective Action	Initials
		Example 200 g / 2 kg	Example 500 g / 4 kg		

Reviewed by (printed name)	Reviewed by (signature)	Date

Scale Verification Log

Date	Scale Being Calibrated	Test Weight		Corrective Action	Initials
		Example 200 g / 2 kg	Example 500 g / 4 kg		

Reviewed by (printed name)	Reviewed by (signature)	Date

Scale Verification Log

Date	Scale Being Calibrated	Test Weight		Corrective Action	Initials
		Example 200 g / 2 kg	Example 500 g / 4 kg		

Reviewed by (printed name)	Reviewed by (signature)	Date

Scale Verification Log

Date	Scale Being Calibrated	Test Weight		Corrective Action	Initials
		Example 200 g / 2 kg	Example 500 g / 4 kg		

Reviewed by (printed name)	Reviewed by (signature)	Date

Scale Verification Log

Date	Scale Being Calibrated	Test Weight		Corrective Action	Initials
		Example 200 g / 2 kg	Example 500 g / 4 kg		

Reviewed by (printed name)	Reviewed by (signature)	Date

Scale Verification Log

Date	Scale Being Calibrated	Test Weight		Corrective Action	Initials
		Example 200 g / 2 kg	Example 500 g / 4 kg		

Reviewed by (printed name)	Reviewed by (signature)	Date

Scale Verification Log

Date	Scale Being Calibrated	Test Weight		Corrective Action	Initials
		Example 200 g / 2 kg	Example 500 g / 4 kg		

Reviewed by (printed name)	Reviewed by (signature)	Date

Scale Verification Log

Date	Scale Being Calibrated	Test Weight		Corrective Action	Initials
		Example 200 g / 2 kg	Example 500 g / 4 kg		

Reviewed by (printed name)	Reviewed by (signature)	Date

Scale Verification Log

Date	Scale Being Calibrated	Test Weight		Corrective Action	Initials
		Example 200 g / 2 kg	Example 500 g / 4 kg		

Reviewed by (printed name)	Reviewed by (signature)	Date

Scale Verification Log

Date	Scale Being Calibrated	Test Weight		Corrective Action	Initials
		Example 200 g / 2 kg	Example 500 g / 4 kg		

Reviewed by (printed name)	Reviewed by (signature)	Date

Scale Verification Log

Date	Scale Being Calibrated	Test Weight		Corrective Action	Initials
		Example 200 g / 2 kg	Example 500 g / 4 kg		

Reviewed by (printed name)	Reviewed by (signature)	Date

Scale Verification Log

Date	Scale Being Calibrated	Test Weight		Corrective Action	Initials
		Example 200 g / 2 kg	Example 500 g / 4 kg		

Reviewed by (printed name)	Reviewed by (signature)	Date

Scale Verification Log

Date	Scale Being Calibrated	Test Weight		Corrective Action	Initials
		Example 200 g / 2 kg	Example 500 g / 4 kg		

Reviewed by (printed name)	Reviewed by (signature)	Date

Scale Verification Log

Date	Scale Being Calibrated	Test Weight		Corrective Action	Initials
		Example 200 g / 2 kg	Example 500 g / 4 kg		

Reviewed by (printed name)	Reviewed by (signature)	Date

Scale Verification Log

Date	Scale Being Calibrated	Test Weight		Corrective Action	Initials
		Example 200 g / 2 kg	Example 500 g / 4 kg		

Reviewed by (printed name)	Reviewed by (signature)	Date

Scale Verification Log

Date	Scale Being Calibrated	Test Weight		Corrective Action	Initials
		Example 200 g / 2 kg	Example 500 g / 4 kg		

Reviewed by (printed name)	Reviewed by (signature)	Date

Scale Verification Log

Date	Scale Being Calibrated	Test Weight		Corrective Action	Initials
		Example 200 g / 2 kg	Example 500 g / 4 kg		

Reviewed by (printed name)	Reviewed by (signature)	Date

Scale Verification Log

Date	Scale Being Calibrated	Test Weight		Corrective Action	Initials
		Example 200 g / 2 kg	Example 500 g / 4 kg		

Reviewed by (printed name)	Reviewed by (signature)	Date

Scale Verification Log

Date	Scale Being Calibrated	Test Weight		Corrective Action	Initials
		Example 200 g / 2 kg	Example 500 g / 4 kg		

Reviewed by (printed name)	Reviewed by (signature)	Date

Scale Verification Log

Date	Scale Being Calibrated	Test Weight		Corrective Action	Initials
		Example 200 g / 2 kg	Example 500 g / 4 kg		

Reviewed by (printed name)	Reviewed by (signature)	Date

Scale Verification Log

Date	Scale Being Calibrated	Test Weight		Corrective Action	Initials
		Example 200 g / 2 kg	Example 500 g / 4 kg		

Reviewed by (printed name)	Reviewed by (signature)	Date

Scale Verification Log

Date	Scale Being Calibrated	Test Weight		Corrective Action	Initials
		Example 200 g / 2 kg	Example 500 g / 4 kg		

Reviewed by (printed name)	Reviewed by (signature)	Date

Scale Verification Log

Date	Scale Being Calibrated	Test Weight		Corrective Action	Initials
		Example 200 g / 2 kg	Example 500 g / 4 kg		

Reviewed by (printed name)	Reviewed by (signature)	Date

Scale Verification Log

Date	Scale Being Calibrated	Test Weight		Corrective Action	Initials
		Example 200 g / 2 kg	Example 500 g / 4 kg		

Reviewed by (printed name)	Reviewed by (signature)	Date

Scale Verification Log

Date	Scale Being Calibrated	Test Weight		Corrective Action	Initials
		Example 200 g / 2 kg	Example 500 g / 4 kg		

Reviewed by (printed name)	Reviewed by (signature)	Date

Scale Verification Log

Date	Scale Being Calibrated	Test Weight		Corrective Action	Initials
		Example 200 g / 2 kg	Example 500 g / 4 kg		

Reviewed by (printed name)	Reviewed by (signature)	Date

Scale Verification Log

Date	Scale Being Calibrated	Test Weight		Corrective Action	Initials
		Example 200 g / 2 kg	Example 500 g / 4 kg		

Reviewed by (printed name)	Reviewed by (signature)	Date

Scale Verification Log

Date	Scale Being Calibrated	Test Weight		Corrective Action	Initials
		Example 200 g / 2 kg	Example 500 g / 4 kg		

Reviewed by (printed name)	Reviewed by (signature)	Date

Scale Verification Log

Date	Scale Being Calibrated	Test Weight		Corrective Action	Initials
		Example 200 g / 2 kg	Example 500 g / 4 kg		

Reviewed by (printed name)	Reviewed by (signature)	Date

Scale Verification Log

Date	Scale Being Calibrated	Test Weight		Corrective Action	Initials
		Example 200 g / 2 kg	Example 500 g / 4 kg		

Reviewed by (printed name)	Reviewed by (signature)	Date

Scale Verification Log

Date	Scale Being Calibrated	Test Weight		Corrective Action	Initials
		Example 200 g / 2 kg	Example 500 g / 4 kg		

Reviewed by (printed name)	Reviewed by (signature)	Date

Scale Verification Log

Date	Scale Being Calibrated	Test Weight		Corrective Action	Initials
		Example 200 g / 2 kg	Example 500 g / 4 kg		

Reviewed by (printed name)	Reviewed by (signature)	Date

Scale Verification Log

Date	Scale Being Calibrated	Test Weight		Corrective Action	Initials
		Example 200 g / 2 kg	Example 500 g / 4 kg		

Reviewed by (printed name)	Reviewed by (signature)	Date

Scale Verification Log

Date	Scale Being Calibrated	Test Weight		Corrective Action	Initials
		Example 200 g / 2 kg	Example 500 g / 4 kg		

Reviewed by (printed name)	Reviewed by (signature)	Date

Scale Verification Log

Date	Scale Being Calibrated	Test Weight		Corrective Action	Initials
		Example 200 g / 2 kg	Example 500 g / 4 kg		

Reviewed by (printed name)	Reviewed by (signature)	Date

Scale Verification Log

Date	Scale Being Calibrated	Test Weight		Corrective Action	Initials
		Example 200 g / 2 kg	Example 500 g / 4 kg		

Reviewed by (printed name)	Reviewed by (signature)	Date

Scale Verification Log

Date	Scale Being Calibrated	Test Weight		Corrective Action	Initials
		Example 200 g / 2 kg	Example 500 g / 4 kg		

Reviewed by (printed name)	Reviewed by (signature)	Date

Scale Verification Log

Date	Scale Being Calibrated	Test Weight		Corrective Action	Initials
		Example 200 g / 2 kg	Example 500 g / 4 kg		

Reviewed by (printed name)	Reviewed by (signature)	Date

Scale Verification Log

Date	Scale Being Calibrated	Test Weight		Corrective Action	Initials
		Example 200 g / 2 kg	Example 500 g / 4 kg		

Reviewed by (printed name)	Reviewed by (signature)	Date

Scale Verification Log

Date	Scale Being Calibrated	Test Weight		Corrective Action	Initials
		Example 200 g / 2 kg	Example 500 g / 4 kg		

Reviewed by (printed name)	Reviewed by (signature)	Date

Scale Verification Log

Date	Scale Being Calibrated	Test Weight		Corrective Action	Initials
		Example 200 g / 2 kg	Example 500 g / 4 kg		

Reviewed by (printed name)	Reviewed by (signature)	Date

Scale Verification Log

Date	Scale Being Calibrated	Test Weight		Corrective Action	Initials
		Example 200 g / 2 kg	Example 500 g / 4 kg		

Reviewed by (printed name)	Reviewed by (signature)	Date

Scale Verification Log

Date	Scale Being Calibrated	Test Weight		Corrective Action	Initials
		Example 200 g / 2 kg	Example 500 g / 4 kg		

Reviewed by (printed name)	Reviewed by (signature)	Date

Scale Verification Log

Date	Scale Being Calibrated	Test Weight		Corrective Action	Initials
		Example 200 g / 2 kg	Example 500 g / 4 kg		

Reviewed by (printed name)	Reviewed by (signature)	Date

Scale Verification Log

Date	Scale Being Calibrated	Test Weight		Corrective Action	Initials
		Example 200 g / 2 kg	Example 500 g / 4 kg		

Reviewed by (printed name)	Reviewed by (signature)	Date

Scale Verification Log

Date	Scale Being Calibrated	Test Weight		Corrective Action	Initials
		Example 200 g / 2 kg	Example 500 g / 4 kg		

Reviewed by (printed name)	Reviewed by (signature)	Date

Scale Verification Log

Date	Scale Being Calibrated	Test Weight		Corrective Action	Initials
		Example 200 g / 2 kg	Example 500 g / 4 kg		

Reviewed by (printed name)	Reviewed by (signature)	Date

Scale Verification Log

Date	Scale Being Calibrated	Test Weight		Corrective Action	Initials
		Example 200 g / 2 kg	Example 500 g / 4 kg		

Reviewed by (printed name)	Reviewed by (signature)	Date

Scale Verification Log

Date	Scale Being Calibrated	Test Weight		Corrective Action	Initials
		Example 200 g / 2 kg	Example 500 g / 4 kg		

Reviewed by (printed name)	Reviewed by (signature)	Date

Scale Verification Log

Date	Scale Being Calibrated	Test Weight		Corrective Action	Initials
		Example 200 g / 2 kg	Example 500 g / 4 kg		

Reviewed by (printed name)	Reviewed by (signature)	Date

Scale Verification Log

Date	Scale Being Calibrated	Test Weight		Corrective Action	Initials
		Example 200 g / 2 kg	Example 500 g / 4 kg		

Reviewed by (printed name)	Reviewed by (signature)	Date

Scale Verification Log

Date	Scale Being Calibrated	Test Weight		Corrective Action	Initials
		Example 200 g / 2 kg	Example 500 g / 4 kg		

Reviewed by (printed name)	Reviewed by (signature)	Date

Scale Verification Log

Date	Scale Being Calibrated	Test Weight		Corrective Action	Initials
		Example 200 g / 2 kg	Example 500 g / 4 kg		

Reviewed by (printed name)	Reviewed by (signature)	Date

Scale Verification Log

Date	Scale Being Calibrated	Test Weight		Corrective Action	Initials
		Example 200 g / 2 kg	Example 500 g / 4 kg		

Reviewed by (printed name)	Reviewed by (signature)	Date

123

Scale Verification Log

Date	Scale Being Calibrated	Test Weight		Corrective Action	Initials
		Example 200 g / 2 kg	Example 500 g / 4 kg		

Reviewed by (printed name)	Reviewed by (signature)	Date

Scale Verification Log

Date	Scale Being Calibrated	Test Weight		Corrective Action	Initials
		Example 200 g / 2 kg	Example 500 g / 4 kg		

Reviewed by (printed name)	Reviewed by (signature)	Date

Scale Verification Log

Date	Scale Being Calibrated	Test Weight		Corrective Action	Initials
		Example 200 g / 2 kg	Example 500 g / 4 kg		

Reviewed by (printed name)	Reviewed by (signature)	Date

Scale Verification Log

Date	Scale Being Calibrated	Test Weight		Corrective Action	Initials
		Example 200 g / 2 kg	Example 500 g / 4 kg		

Reviewed by (printed name)	Reviewed by (signature)	Date

Scale Verification Log

Date	Scale Being Calibrated	Test Weight		Corrective Action	Initials
		Example 200 g / 2 kg	Example 500 g / 4 kg		

Reviewed by (printed name)	Reviewed by (signature)	Date

Scale Verification Log

Date	Scale Being Calibrated	Test Weight		Corrective Action	Initials
		Example 200 g / 2 kg	Example 500 g / 4 kg		

Reviewed by (printed name)	Reviewed by (signature)	Date

Scale Verification Log

Date	Scale Being Calibrated	Test Weight		Corrective Action	Initials
		Example 200 g / 2 kg	Example 500 g / 4 kg		

Reviewed by (printed name)	Reviewed by (signature)	Date

Scale Verification Log

Date	Scale Being Calibrated	Test Weight		Corrective Action	Initials
		Example 200 g / 2 kg	Example 500 g / 4 kg		

Reviewed by (printed name)	Reviewed by (signature)	Date

Scale Verification Log

Date	Scale Being Calibrated	Test Weight		Corrective Action	Initials
		Example 200 g / 2 kg	Example 500 g / 4 kg		

Reviewed by (printed name)	Reviewed by (signature)	Date

Scale Verification Log

Date	Scale Being Calibrated	Test Weight		Corrective Action	Initials
		Example 200 g / 2 kg	Example 500 g / 4 kg		

Reviewed by (printed name)	Reviewed by (signature)	Date

Scale Verification Log

Date	Scale Being Calibrated	Test Weight		Corrective Action	Initials
		Example 200 g / 2 kg	Example 500 g / 4 kg		

Reviewed by (printed name)	Reviewed by (signature)	Date

Scale Verification Log

Date	Scale Being Calibrated	Test Weight		Corrective Action	Initials
		Example 200 g / 2 kg	Example 500 g / 4 kg		

Reviewed by (printed name)	Reviewed by (signature)	Date

Scale Verification Log

Date	Scale Being Calibrated	Test Weight		Corrective Action	Initials
		Example 200 g / 2 kg	Example 500 g / 4 kg		

Reviewed by (printed name)	Reviewed by (signature)	Date

Scale Verification Log

Date	Scale Being Calibrated	Test Weight		Corrective Action	Initials
		Example 200 g / 2 kg	Example 500 g / 4 kg		

Reviewed by (printed name)	Reviewed by (signature)	Date

Scale Verification Log

Date	Scale Being Calibrated	Test Weight		Corrective Action	Initials
		Example 200 g / 2 kg	Example 500 g / 4 kg		

Reviewed by (printed name)	Reviewed by (signature)	Date

Scale Verification Log

Date	Scale Being Calibrated	Test Weight		Corrective Action	Initials
		Example 200 g / 2 kg	Example 500 g / 4 kg		

Reviewed by (printed name)	Reviewed by (signature)	Date

Scale Verification Log

Date	Scale Being Calibrated	Test Weight		Corrective Action	Initials
		Example 200 g / 2 kg	Example 500 g / 4 kg		

Reviewed by (printed name)	Reviewed by (signature)	Date

Scale Verification Log

Date	Scale Being Calibrated	Test Weight		Corrective Action	Initials
		Example 200 g / 2 kg	Example 500 g / 4 kg		

Reviewed by (printed name)	Reviewed by (signature)	Date

Scale Verification Log

Date	Scale Being Calibrated	Test Weight		Corrective Action	Initials
		Example 200 g / 2 kg	Example 500 g / 4 kg		

Reviewed by (printed name)	Reviewed by (signature)	Date

Scale Verification Log

Date	Scale Being Calibrated	Test Weight		Corrective Action	Initials
		Example 200 g / 2 kg	Example 500 g / 4 kg		

Reviewed by (printed name)	Reviewed by (signature)	Date

Scale Verification Log

Date	Scale Being Calibrated	Test Weight		Corrective Action	Initials
		Example 200 g / 2 kg	Example 500 g / 4 kg		

Reviewed by (printed name)	Reviewed by (signature)	Date

Scale Verification Log

Date	Scale Being Calibrated	Test Weight		Corrective Action	Initials
		Example 200 g / 2 kg	Example 500 g / 4 kg		

Reviewed by (printed name)	Reviewed by (signature)	Date

Scale Verification Log

Date	Scale Being Calibrated	Test Weight		Corrective Action	Initials
		Example 200 g / 2 kg	Example 500 g / 4 kg		

Reviewed by (printed name)	Reviewed by (signature)	Date

Scale Verification Log

Date	Scale Being Calibrated	Test Weight		Corrective Action	Initials
		Example 200 g / 2 kg	Example 500 g / 4 kg		

Reviewed by (printed name)	Reviewed by (signature)	Date

Scale Verification Log

Date	Scale Being Calibrated	Test Weight		Corrective Action	Initials
		Example 200 g / 2 kg	Example 500 g / 4 kg		

Reviewed by (printed name)	Reviewed by (signature)	Date

Scale Verification Log

Date	Scale Being Calibrated	Test Weight		Corrective Action	Initials
		Example 200 g / 2 kg	Example 500 g / 4 kg		

Reviewed by (printed name)	Reviewed by (signature)	Date

Scale Verification Log

Date	Scale Being Calibrated	Test Weight		Corrective Action	Initials
		Example 200 g / 2 kg	Example 500 g / 4 kg		

Reviewed by (printed name)	Reviewed by (signature)	Date

Scale Verification Log

Date	Scale Being Calibrated	Test Weight		Corrective Action	Initials
		Example 200 g / 2 kg	Example 500 g / 4 kg		

Reviewed by (printed name)	Reviewed by (signature)	Date

Scale Verification Log

Date	Scale Being Calibrated	Test Weight		Corrective Action	Initials
		Example 200 g / 2 kg	Example 500 g / 4 kg		

Reviewed by (printed name)	Reviewed by (signature)	Date

Scale Verification Log

Date	Scale Being Calibrated	Test Weight		Corrective Action	Initials
		Example 200 g / 2 kg	Example 500 g / 4 kg		

Reviewed by (printed name)	Reviewed by (signature)	Date

Scale Verification Log

Date	Scale Being Calibrated	Test Weight		Corrective Action	Initials
		Example 200 g / 2 kg	Example 500 g / 4 kg		

Reviewed by (printed name)	Reviewed by (signature)	Date

Scale Verification Log

Date	Scale Being Calibrated	Test Weight		Corrective Action	Initials
		Example 200 g / 2 kg	Example 500 g / 4 kg		

Reviewed by (printed name)	Reviewed by (signature)	Date

155

Scale Verification Log

Date	Scale Being Calibrated	Test Weight		Corrective Action	Initials
		Example 200 g / 2 kg	Example 500 g / 4 kg		

Reviewed by (printed name)	Reviewed by (signature)	Date

Scale Verification Log

Date	Scale Being Calibrated	Test Weight		Corrective Action	Initials
		Example 200 g / 2 kg	Example 500 g / 4 kg		

Reviewed by (printed name)	Reviewed by (signature)	Date

Scale Verification Log

Date	Scale Being Calibrated	Test Weight		Corrective Action	Initials
		Example 200 g / 2 kg	Example 500 g / 4 kg		

Reviewed by (printed name)	Reviewed by (signature)	Date

Scale Verification Log

Date	Scale Being Calibrated	Test Weight		Corrective Action	Initials
		Example 200 g / 2 kg	Example 500 g / 4 kg		

Reviewed by (printed name)	Reviewed by (signature)	Date

Scale Verification Log

Date	Scale Being Calibrated	Test Weight		Corrective Action	Initials
		Example 200 g / 2 kg	Example 500 g / 4 kg		

Reviewed by (printed name)	Reviewed by (signature)	Date

Scale Verification Log

Date	Scale Being Calibrated	Test Weight		Corrective Action	Initials
		Example 200 g / 2 kg	Example 500 g / 4 kg		

Reviewed by (printed name)	Reviewed by (signature)	Date

Scale Verification Log

Date	Scale Being Calibrated	Test Weight		Corrective Action	Initials
		Example 200 g / 2 kg	Example 500 g / 4 kg		

Reviewed by (printed name)	Reviewed by (signature)	Date

Scale Verification Log

Date	Scale Being Calibrated	Test Weight		Corrective Action	Initials
		Example 200 g / 2 kg	Example 500 g / 4 kg		

Reviewed by (printed name)	Reviewed by (signature)	Date

Scale Verification Log

Date	Scale Being Calibrated	Test Weight		Corrective Action	Initials
		Example 200 g / 2 kg	Example 500 g / 4 kg		

Reviewed by (printed name)	Reviewed by (signature)	Date

Scale Verification Log

Date	Scale Being Calibrated	Test Weight		Corrective Action	Initials
		Example 200 g / 2 kg	Example 500 g / 4 kg		

Reviewed by (printed name)	Reviewed by (signature)	Date

Scale Verification Log

Date	Scale Being Calibrated	Test Weight		Corrective Action	Initials
		Example 200 g / 2 kg	Example 500 g / 4 kg		

Reviewed by (printed name)	Reviewed by (signature)	Date

Scale Verification Log

Date	Scale Being Calibrated	Test Weight		Corrective Action	Initials
		Example 200 g / 2 kg	Example 500 g / 4 kg		

Reviewed by (printed name)	Reviewed by (signature)	Date

Scale Verification Log

Date	Scale Being Calibrated	Test Weight		Corrective Action	Initials
		Example 200 g / 2 kg	Example 500 g / 4 kg		

Reviewed by (printed name)	Reviewed by (signature)	Date

Scale Verification Log

Date	Scale Being Calibrated	Test Weight		Corrective Action	Initials
		Example 200 g / 2 kg	Example 500 g / 4 kg		

Reviewed by (printed name)	Reviewed by (signature)	Date

Scale Verification Log

Date	Scale Being Calibrated	Test Weight		Corrective Action	Initials
		Example 200 g / 2 kg	Example 500 g / 4 kg		

Reviewed by (printed name)	Reviewed by (signature)	Date

Scale Verification Log

Date	Scale Being Calibrated	Test Weight		Corrective Action	Initials
		Example 200 g / 2 kg	Example 500 g / 4 kg		

Reviewed by (printed name)	Reviewed by (signature)	Date

Scale Verification Log

Date	Scale Being Calibrated	Test Weight		Corrective Action	Initials
		Example 200 g / 2 kg	Example 500 g / 4 kg		

Reviewed by (printed name)	Reviewed by (signature)	Date

Scale Verification Log

Date	Scale Being Calibrated	Test Weight		Corrective Action	Initials
		Example 200 g / 2 kg	Example 500 g / 4 kg		

Reviewed by (printed name)	Reviewed by (signature)	Date

Scale Verification Log

Date	Scale Being Calibrated	Test Weight		Corrective Action	Initials
		Example 200 g / 2 kg	Example 500 g / 4 kg		

Reviewed by (printed name)	Reviewed by (signature)	Date

Scale Verification Log

Date	Scale Being Calibrated	Test Weight Example 200 g / 2 kg	Example 500 g / 4 kg	Corrective Action	Initials

Reviewed by (printed name)	Reviewed by (signature)	Date

Scale Verification Log

Date	Scale Being Calibrated	Test Weight		Corrective Action	Initials
		Example 200 g / 2 kg	Example 500 g / 4 kg		

Reviewed by (printed name)	Reviewed by (signature)	Date

Scale Verification Log

Date	Scale Being Calibrated	Test Weight		Corrective Action	Initials
		Example 200 g / 2 kg	Example 500 g / 4 kg		

Reviewed by (printed name)	Reviewed by (signature)	Date

Scale Verification Log

Date	Scale Being Calibrated	Test Weight		Corrective Action	Initials
		Example 200 g / 2 kg	Example 500 g / 4 kg		

Reviewed by (printed name)	Reviewed by (signature)	Date

Scale Verification Log

Date	Scale Being Calibrated	Test Weight		Corrective Action	Initials
		Example 200 g / 2 kg	Example 500 g / 4 kg		

Reviewed by (printed name)	Reviewed by (signature)	Date

Scale Verification Log

Date	Scale Being Calibrated	Test Weight		Corrective Action	Initials
		Example 200 g / 2 kg	Example 500 g / 4 kg		

Reviewed by (printed name)	Reviewed by (signature)	Date

Scale Verification Log

Date	Scale Being Calibrated	Test Weight		Corrective Action	Initials
		Example 200 g / 2 kg	Example 500 g / 4 kg		

Reviewed by (printed name)	Reviewed by (signature)	Date

Scale Verification Log

Date	Scale Being Calibrated	Test Weight		Corrective Action	Initials
		Example 200 g / 2 kg	Example 500 g / 4 kg		

Reviewed by (printed name)	Reviewed by (signature)	Date

Scale Verification Log

Date	Scale Being Calibrated	Test Weight		Corrective Action	Initials
		Example 200 g / 2 kg	Example 500 g / 4 kg		

Reviewed by (printed name)	Reviewed by (signature)	Date

Scale Verification Log

Date	Scale Being Calibrated	Test Weight		Corrective Action	Initials
		Example 200 g / 2 kg	Example 500 g / 4 kg		

Reviewed by (printed name)	Reviewed by (signature)	Date

Scale Verification Log

Date	Scale Being Calibrated	Test Weight		Corrective Action	Initials
		Example 200 g / 2 kg	Example 500 g / 4 kg		

Reviewed by (printed name)	Reviewed by (signature)	Date

Scale Verification Log

Date	Scale Being Calibrated	Test Weight		Corrective Action	Initials
		Example 200 g / 2 kg	Example 500 g / 4 kg		

Reviewed by (printed name)	Reviewed by (signature)	Date

Scale Verification Log

Date	Scale Being Calibrated	Test Weight		Corrective Action	Initials
		Example 200 g / 2 kg	Example 500 g / 4 kg		

Reviewed by (printed name)	Reviewed by (signature)	Date

Scale Verification Log

Date	Scale Being Calibrated	Test Weight		Corrective Action	Initials
		Example 200 g / 2 kg	Example 500 g / 4 kg		

Reviewed by (printed name)	Reviewed by (signature)	Date

Scale Verification Log

Date	Scale Being Calibrated	Test Weight		Corrective Action	Initials
		Example 200 g / 2 kg	Example 500 g / 4 kg		

Reviewed by (printed name)	Reviewed by (signature)	Date

Scale Verification Log

Date	Scale Being Calibrated	Test Weight		Corrective Action	Initials
		Example 200 g / 2 kg	Example 500 g / 4 kg		

Reviewed by (printed name)	Reviewed by (signature)	Date

Scale Verification Log

Date	Scale Being Calibrated	Test Weight		Corrective Action	Initials
		Example 200 g / 2 kg	Example 500 g / 4 kg		

Reviewed by (printed name)	Reviewed by (signature)	Date

Scale Verification Log

Date	Scale Being Calibrated	Test Weight		Corrective Action	Initials
		Example 200 g / 2 kg	Example 500 g / 4 kg		

Reviewed by (printed name)	Reviewed by (signature)	Date

Scale Verification Log

Date	Scale Being Calibrated	Test Weight		Corrective Action	Initials
		Example 200 g / 2 kg	Example 500 g / 4 kg		

Reviewed by (printed name)	Reviewed by (signature)	Date

Scale Verification Log

Date	Scale Being Calibrated	Test Weight		Corrective Action	Initials
		Example 200 g / 2 kg	Example 500 g / 4 kg		

Reviewed by (printed name)	Reviewed by (signature)	Date

Scale Verification Log

Date	Scale Being Calibrated	Test Weight		Corrective Action	Initials
		Example 200 g / 2 kg	Example 500 g / 4 kg		

Reviewed by (printed name)	Reviewed by (signature)	Date

Scale Verification Log

Date	Scale Being Calibrated	Test Weight		Corrective Action	Initials
		Example 200 g / 2 kg	Example 500 g / 4 kg		

Reviewed by (printed name)	Reviewed by (signature)	Date

Scale Verification Log

Date	Scale Being Calibrated	Test Weight		Corrective Action	Initials
		Example 200 g / 2 kg	Example 500 g / 4 kg		

Reviewed by (printed name)	Reviewed by (signature)	Date

Scale Verification Log

Date	Scale Being Calibrated	Test Weight		Corrective Action	Initials
		Example 200 g / 2 kg	Example 500 g / 4 kg		

Reviewed by (printed name)	Reviewed by (signature)	Date

Scale Verification Log

Date	Scale Being Calibrated	Test Weight		Corrective Action	Initials
		Example 200 g / 2 kg	Example 500 g / 4 kg		

Reviewed by (printed name)	Reviewed by (signature)	Date

Scale Verification Log

Date	Scale Being Calibrated	Test Weight		Corrective Action	Initials
		Example 200 g / 2 kg	Example 500 g / 4 kg		

Reviewed by (printed name)	Reviewed by (signature)	Date

Scale Verification Log

Date	Scale Being Calibrated	Test Weight		Corrective Action	Initials
		Example 200 g / 2 kg	Example 500 g / 4 kg		

Reviewed by (printed name)	Reviewed by (signature)	Date

Scale Verification Log

Date	Scale Being Calibrated	Test Weight		Corrective Action	Initials
		Example 200 g / 2 kg	Example 500 g / 4 kg		

Reviewed by (printed name)	Reviewed by (signature)	Date

Scale Verification Log

Date	Scale Being Calibrated	Test Weight		Corrective Action	Initials
		Example 200 g / 2 kg	Example 500 g / 4 kg		

Reviewed by (printed name)	Reviewed by (signature)	Date

Scale Verification Log

Date	Scale Being Calibrated	Test Weight		Corrective Action	Initials
		Example 200 g / 2 kg	Example 500 g / 4 kg		

Reviewed by (printed name)	Reviewed by (signature)	Date

Scale Verification Log

Date	Scale Being Calibrated	Test Weight		Corrective Action	Initials
		Example 200 g / 2 kg	Example 500 g / 4 kg		

Reviewed by (printed name)	Reviewed by (signature)	Date

Scale Verification Log

Date	Scale Being Calibrated	Test Weight		Corrective Action	Initials
		Example 200 g / 2 kg	Example 500 g / 4 kg		

Reviewed by (printed name)	Reviewed by (signature)	Date

Scale Verification Log

Date	Scale Being Calibrated	Test Weight		Corrective Action	Initials
		Example 200 g / 2 kg	Example 500 g / 4 kg		

Reviewed by (printed name)	Reviewed by (signature)	Date

Scale Verification Log

Date	Scale Being Calibrated	Test Weight		Corrective Action	Initials
		Example 200 g / 2 kg	Example 500 g / 4 kg		

Reviewed by (printed name)	Reviewed by (signature)	Date

Scale Verification Log

Date	Scale Being Calibrated	Test Weight		Corrective Action	Initials
		Example 200 g / 2 kg	Example 500 g / 4 kg		

Reviewed by (printed name)	Reviewed by (signature)	Date

Scale Verification Log

Date	Scale Being Calibrated	Test Weight		Corrective Action	Initials
		Example 200 g / 2 kg	Example 500 g / 4 kg		

Reviewed by (printed name)	Reviewed by (signature)	Date

Scale Verification Log

Date	Scale Being Calibrated	Test Weight		Corrective Action	Initials
		Example 200 g / 2 kg	Example 500 g / 4 kg		

Reviewed by (printed name)	Reviewed by (signature)	Date